TWO WRONGS DON'T MAKE A RIGHT AND OTHER STORIES

Arohi Patil

MEDIA PA

Copyright

Design & Layout by Prem Puthur
Printed in the United States of America
ISBN 978-0-9895698-3-5
Published by BRPBooks
307 Woodridge Lane
Media
PA 19063

This book is for my mother and my father.

Author's Note

All characters, names and places in this book are fictional and the work of imagination. Any resemblance to any person living or dead would be purely coincidental and not intentional.

Acknowledgements

I'm thankful to my parents, grandparents, my siblings, my aunts, uncles, cousins and special thanks to Prem uncle for making this book a reality.

I'm also thankful to Dennis De Rose my editor for doing a wonderful job of editing my stories.

Also special thanks to my sister, Adwaita for her beautiful illustrations.

Prelude

All stories are meant to entertain and help children think positive and learn to help others when needed.

Contents

Story 1

Bubbles - The Savior

Onia, a courageous nine-year-old girl, was looking forward to going on her next fishing trip with Chimpu, her father. He was a fisherman and she helped out whenever she could. Onia was cheerful and full of life. She loved sailing and fishing. Actually, Onia loved salty water splashing on her face. Weird, but she liked the taste of salty water too. She would dive into the ocean whenever her dad would permit it. The ocean was too rough and choppy most of the time but there were a few safe places to swim. She was an expert swimmer. She always had different stories to tell to her many friends after her fishing trips. She was really good at telling stories. She made them interesting and humorous.

When they finally set sail, they caught something big in the net. "Oh boy," she said, "it's a baby whale!" Her father was sleeping below so she decided not to wake him. "I should let him go," she said to herself. She went to the net, looked at the whale and felt really bad; it looked so helpless hanging there. The whale was struggling, looking at Onia as if he wanted Onia to help him escape. Immediately, Onia lowered the net back into the water, the whale slowly worked his way out.

"Come and sit on my back," the whale said to Onia. "I'll take you around for a fun ride."

"Okay," Onia said, "but first let me rearrange the net, hook it back on the machine and lower it into the water so we can catch more fish." After Onia did what she had to do, she sat on the whale's back with anticipation. The whale swam fast but made sure that Onia didn't fall off. Every time he squirted water from his blowhole, Onia went flying into the air, coming down with a thump on the whale's back. It was lots of fun and Onia was having the time of her life. They became best friends very quickly. The whale protected her while she was in his care. They enjoyed being together. Onia played with the whale for a long time; suddenly she remembered that she had to return to the ship before her father woke up.

She climbed up the boat's ladder but as soon as her dad saw her, he shouted, "Where were you, you silly girl?" He didn't even wait for her answer before he continued, "Where did you go? Do you know how worried I was?" He hugged her and kissed her over and over before she could even answer him. When the storm settled, she explained the whole story to him. He took a deep breath and sighed, "I'm glad you are back safe and sound." Together, they pulled the net in and found lots of fish inside. They went home and sold their fish at the market for a very good price.

The next day, when they were getting ready to go out fishing, Onia heard people shouting, "Help, help, a boy is drowning." Onia ran toward the crowd and without wasting any time, she jumped into the water. She grabbed the drowning child; the force of the water was too strong for her. It smashed at them; they went under the water very quickly. Onia realized they weren't going to survive but she refused to let go of the boy to try and save herself. Soon, they both disappeared completely, below the surface of the water. Immediately, someone from the crowd said, "Onia should not have dived in. She should have known better. This is the roughest part of the ocean. No one has ever dived in here and survived to tell about it." The villagers felt sad, many began to cry.

Suddenly, someone said, "Look, it's Onia; she has the boy with her."
"That's a miracle!" someone else said.

"I think she is sitting on the back of a young whale, isn't she?"
"Yes, she is indeed," Onia's father said happily.

When Onia came out of water, her father kissed her again and again and said, "I'm proud of you and your friend, the whale who saved you." From that day onward, the whale never left the rough waters and has saved the lives of many drowning children. Onia goes on special rides with Bubbles frequently. She named her friend – Bubbles; the villagers call him, 'The Savior'. Cool, isn't it?

Story 2

It Doesn't Hurt to Listen

Naomi is a beautiful nine-year-old girl. She is very creative, composes beautiful poems, loves to eat healthy food and play with her brother and sister. But she has one very bad habit. She always tells everyone to "shut up." She doesn't care who she's talking to or what they're saying to her, her immediate response is always "shut up".

One day, she was playing with her puppy, tossing him up in the air. When her mother saw what she was doing, her mother said, "Naomi, don't do that, your puppy may fall and get hurt."

She immediately replied, "You shut up, Mom."

Just then, her puppy slipped out of her hands, hit the ground and was badly hurt. Her mother had to rush the puppy to the veterinarian. The veterinarian said that puppy's leg was fractured and needed immediate treatment. Naomi's parents did not allow Naomi to play with her puppy for a very long time after that. She missed playing with her puppy a lot because she loved him very much. She said, "I'm sorry," to her puppy and her parents many times. But did she really mean it? No. She continued to repeat her old behavior, nothing had changed.

Another time, when she was climbing a tree in her backyard while her grandfather was raking leaves nearby, he said, "Naomi, be careful! Don't climb on the small branches. You may fall."

She responded, "Shut up, Grandpa."

As soon as her grandfather got back to work, he heard a loud thump. He immediately knew what had happened. Naomi was on the ground, crying for help. Worried, he rushed to help her. He picked her up. She was in terrible pain. He checked her body to see whether any bones were broken. He was relieved when he realized that no bones were broken. However, she was bruised all over and had minor cuts, all extremely painful. But did she learn her lesson?

She loved playing around the house, opening doors and slamming them behind her was one of her favorite games. Her grandmother was concerned that she would get hurt. So her grandmother said, "Naomi, be careful when you close those doors, you may hurt your hand."

"You shut up, Grandma," Naomi said, as usual, as she continued to slam doors behind her. As soon as she said that, her hand got caught in the door, she couldn't use her hand for three days; it hurt too much to even move it.

One Sunday, she was playing on the swing. She was going very high, while swinging without even holding on to the chains. So her father said, "Naomi be careful, you may fall and get hurt."

"Shut up, Papa," Naomi responded automatically.

So her dad left her alone and went inside the house. Shortly after that, he looked outside, he saw Naomi lying on the

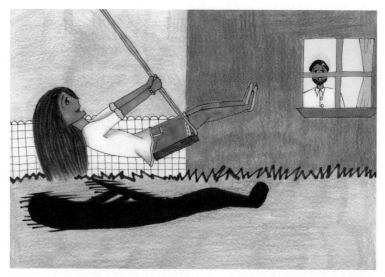

ground, crying for help. He rushed outside to help her. She was in pain; she wasn't able to move her right arm. He drove her to the emergency room at the hospital. The doctor found out that her shoulder was dislocated. He needed to put her shoulder back in place. When he did that, it hurt a lot but Naomi still didn't learn her lesson.

That same winter, it snowed heavily. Kids from the neighborhood were playing in the snow. Naomi wanted to play with them. When she was about to step outside, Saloni, her older sister, said, "Naomi, you need to put on your snow boots and a heavy coat."

Naomi said, "Saloni, Shut up," and ran out the door without minding her sister.

That same day, the bitter cold made her very sick. Her parents had to rush her to the hospital once again. After a short wait, the doctor said, "She has pneumonia."

She had to spend more than a week in the hospital. She didn't like the hospital food and she hated injections. She felt awful; she was missing all the winter fun. As soon as she got home, she wanted to go outside and play. Her parents told her that the doctor said it would take several more days for her to get better. She remained indoors for several more weeks. She had a lot of time to think and she finally learned her lesson. Thereafter, she stopped telling everyone to 'shut up' and she began to listen to others.

Now she is fun to be around, has learned a lot and is more creative in her activities. She also writes beautiful stories to children explaining the benefits of good behavior.

Story 3

Lila and the Golden Coin

Lila needed to fetch a bucket of water for her mother. She followed the path that led to the well. She lowered the bucket into the well, when it was full, she pulled it up. To her surprise, she found a shimmering golden coin at the bottom of the bucket. Lila's family was very poor. Lila knew her family really needed the coin. She hurried home, carefully avoiding spilling the water. When she got home, she quickly handed the bucket to her mother and held up the coin, "Mom, look what I found."

Her mother looked at the coin and exclaimed, "Wow! You are a lucky girl."

"What do you want me to do with the coin, Mom?" Lila flipped the coin into the air. The sun touched the coin and it glowed brilliantly.

"Since you found it, it's yours to keep or spend. You can go to the market tomorrow and buy something for yourself," her mother responded.

"What should I buy, Mom?" She was excited, thinking about all the things she could buy with one gold coin.

"I'm sure they'll have some sweets that you like. But now you had better get some sleep. It looks like you're going to have a busy day tomorrow."

Early in the morning, Lila got ready and headed for the market. The market wasn't far from her house. Once there, she noticed a variety of sweets, just like her mother had said. She also saw lots of toys and a little necklace that she had always wanted. She immediately decided to buy it. Then she remembered that there wasn't anything in the house to eat. She remembered that her mother hadn't eaten in two days, so she realized that buying the necklace would be a selfish thing to do. Immediately, she left the market and found a grocery store. As she was about to buy groceries, she saw a wrinkled old man sitting nearby with his hands held out, palms up.

"Oh please, give me some money or something to eat? No one has given me anything at all today," the old man pleaded with her.

Lila turned toward him and looked at his hands. They were empty. She knew what she had to do. Lila walked over to the old man and quickly dropped the gold coin in his hands, smiling warmly. The old man thanked her. On her way back home, Lila thought about the old man; she felt good that she was able to help him.

As soon as Lila reached home, her mom asked, "Lila, what did you buy at the market?"

Lila told her mom what she did with the coin. Her mom was very pleased and proud of her little daughter. Her mother hugged her tightly.

The next day, Lila went to school feeling very happy. "Today, we will be learning division," the teacher told the class. When the bell rang, Lila packed up, waved goodbye to all her friends and headed home. As soon as she reached home, she hurriedly washed herself with a bucketful of water and sat down to complete her homework. While she was doing her homework, she heard a knock on the door. She got up and opened the door. To her astonishment, she saw the same old man standing in the doorway.

"Hello," she said.

"Hello," he replied.

"What are you doing here?"

"I just came to see you," the old man said.

"What can I do for you?" she asked politely.

"I have come here to return your coin." He forced the golden coin and a necklace into her hands.

"Why are you returning the coin? I gave you the coin because you needed it. Where did you find this necklace?"

"I purchased the necklace that you wanted and this coin isn't just an ordinary coin," he said. "It's a special coin. You need it more than I do." Then he left.

The next day, when Lila woke up, she found two coins lying where she had placed the original one. On the third day, there were four. The next day there were eight. They were doubling each day. The pattern continued. A few days later, Lila went to the market, hoping to find the old man. Surprisingly, he was sitting near the market, asking for help. She wanted to find out about him and the coin. "Oh, my dear, you won't be able to figure out who I'm," he said.

" Are you a magician?" Lila asked.

He smiled and then said, "I test people, but so far, only you have passed the test. Several people come to the market, buying more than they need. No one wants to give me anything. They ignore me even when I call out to them for help. They are always too busy shopping. The other day, when I asked you to give me something, you immediately walked up to me and gave me the only coin you had. You wanted that necklace so badly, but you still didn't buy it. Then you thought of buying groceries for your family, but you didn't buy the groceries either, and you gave me your only coin, a precious gold coin."

"How did you know what I was thinking?" Lila asked, surprised by his statement.

He smiled his mysterious smile again. "I was glad that you didn't allow your need to hold you back from helping me."

"Who put that golden coin in that bucket?" she asked.

"I did." The old man smiled mysteriously once more.

"Thank you for everything," Lila said.

"That coin will be yours as long as you continue helping others. But the moment you stop helping others, you will lose the coin." The old man got up and left.

Lila still has the coin in her possession.

Story 4

The Real Champion

There was a tiny village situated at the bottom of the Sahyadri Mountains, it was called Pali. An extremely poor family of five lived in the village - a mother, a father, two-year-old twins (a boy and a girl) and their older sister, Natasha. Natasha loved to play in the woods behind their hut. Natasha's family wasn't able to afford a decent house like the other villagers so they built their own hut out of sticks and stones and whatever they found along the banks of the river.

It was very difficult for Natasha's family to survive. Natasha would go around the village looking for any kind of work. Usually, she would get a rupee or two for doing chores for others. Many times, Natasha's family had nothing to eat. Natasha was getting used to sleeping without eating anything. But the twins would cry all night, keeping everyone awake. They were turning into cranky kids. Natasha's parents fought frequently because they didn't know how to handle their situation. They were so poor; they couldn't take the kids to see the doctor even when the kids were really sick.

One day, when the temperature was over 96 degrees, everyone was feeling awfully hot, except the rich, they could afford fans and air-conditioners. Natasha and her parents decided to go to the stream to cool off. The stream was in the woods. The villagers called it the 'Freezing Stream' because the water was always very cold. Since it was 96 degrees, the water wasn't that cold. So Natasha's family started trudging up the knoll that banked the stream on the other side. But when they got to the top of the hill, one of the twins slipped and tumbled into the stream on the other side. The mother began to cry, the father was so beside himself; he didn't know what to do. He couldn't even think clearly enough to run down the stream and grab the child as she floated past him. As always, Natasha thought quickly and acted swiftly. She knew she only had one option and had to act quickly. So she rolled into the stream as fast as a black

commando. She was exceptionally skilled at rolling. When she realized that her sister was drowning, she turned pale but quickly mustered her courage, she ducked under the water and grabbed her sister, brought her to the surface of the water and dragged her to the edge of the bank.

Luckily, the water was shallower near the edge of the bank. When Natasha heard her sister crying from fright, she felt relieved. Her father came running down, grabbed his child and held her in his arms. Quickly, he checked her body for bruises or broken bones. Carefully, he passed the little girl to his wife. Natasha's mother sat down with both twins in her lap, feeling relieved; she kissed them again and again. She wiped the girl with a piece of her clothing. The whole family was thankful that the child was safe. Natasha was happy because she was able to save her baby sister. Her family thought she was a Real Champion.

Later that evening, Natasha went into the village to see if she could get any work. While walking around the village, she noticed an old man sitting in the door of his hut. Natasha walked over to the old man and asked, "Do you need any help with anything?"

"Yes! If you do some chores for me, I will give you something special," he replied.

Immediately, Natasha started sweeping the floors. Then she cleaned everything inside the hut. She went in the garden, planted roses, violets, daffodils, rosemary, buttercups and daisies. She continued to work for him as needed. So one day, the old man gave Natasha a lemon tree. He said, "This lemon tree will help you tremendously."

Natasha took the lemon tree home and showed it to her family. Later, she planted the tree behind their hut. The next day, to her amazement, she saw that the plant was fully grown and had hundreds of lemons on it. Happily, Natasha told her family to come outside and look at the tree. They were all very surprised. They started picking lemons off the tree with grins on their faces. Whenever they plucked a lemon, another lemon grew back in its place instantly. Day after day, the family would go to the market and sell the lemons. They also began making delicious pickles out of the lemons and selling them in the market. Even after they became rich, Natasha didn't ignore the poor. She would give poor people lemons and pickles for free. Every time she helped others, she felt truly happy and became more determined to help them. After that, Natasha's family  never had to struggle. They had lots of money and their hearts were lighter.

Sharing with others brought real joy in their lives. No one ever left Natasha's house without feeling happy.

Story 5

The Loyal Dogs

Sonia didn't like school because everyone always picked on her. Her parents were very poor; they couldn't afford to buy her new clothes. All the other children in her class wore new clothes frequently. She wore torn old clothes and walked barefoot. Her classmates teased her and said hurtful things to her. They were never nice to her. They pushed her and called her names. She hated going to school because she was tired of her classmates always saying mean things to her. She didn't know how to deal with them. She looked forward to weekends so she could be with her best friends, Rocky and Jacky. They were the best dogs in the world. They had the finest sense of smell and were excellent watchdogs. They were well groomed and their playfulness attracted others easily. Sonia loved having them around; unfortunately she wasn't allowed to bring them to school. She missed them very much while she was in school. Her uncle Gary had given them to her on her third birthday; they were only puppies at the time. Sonia played with them from the time she got up until the time she went to bed. They followed her everywhere; they became very fond and protective of Sonia. Her father, Andre, trained them well.

They even learned to chase crooks and strangers who hang around the house. One night, when Sonia and her parents were sleeping, two thieves entered their home through an open window. Rocky and Jacky smelled them and caught them by surprise. Confused, the thieves began to run away but

the dogs chased them. Before the dogs could catch them, the thieves somehow managed to climb the nearest tree. When dogs realized that they weren't able to get them, they began to bark as loudly as they could. When Sonia's parents heard the dogs barking and men shouting for help, they came outside, rushing to see what was going on. Sonia followed them. She was happy to see that her dear dogs were safe. One of the neighbors ran to the police station and returned with two police officers. When the police officers saw the thieves, one of them said to Sonia's parents, "We have been trying to catch these crooks for a very long time, but we were never able to catch them. We are truly grateful to Rocky and Jacky." The police officers arrested the thieves and threw them in their van. Before leaving the premises, the crooks looked at the dogs angrily. But the dogs didn't even notice it. They were busy licking Sonia's hands continuously. They seemed to be glad that Sonia was safe as well. She hugged Rocky and Jacky several times and said to them, "You guys are the best!"

The next day, the villagers found out that the cops had recovered lots of gold, jewelry, watches, money and other items. The robbers had stolen a huge amount of money and different items over a period of time from several families. The villagers were happy to receive their things back and were proud to have Rocky and Jacky in their village.

Now, everyone's attitude toward Sonia has changed. Suddenly, children in school have started to say nice things to her. Many of them, those who didn't want to be friends with her in the past or said bad things to her, want to be friends with her now. Now they say things like 'you have the coolest dogs' or 'your dogs are awesome.' She never hated anyone or held a grudge. When they asked her to be  their friend, she readily accepted their friendship. Sonia was no longer lonely at school. Nobody picked on her anymore. She looked forward to going to school and enjoyed playing with her classmates.

In the meantime, another good thing happened to Sonia's family. The police awarded them $10,000 for their assistance in catching the crooks. Now Sonia's parents have enough money to buy basic things, including a new phone in the house.

One evening, when Sonia was at home, the phone rang.

"Hello is this Sonia?" the caller asked, as if he knew her personally.

"Yes."

"I'm calling from the police station. May I talk to your father?"

Sonia handed the receiver to her dad. "This is Sonia's dad. How may I help you?"

"Hello, Mr. Jackson. I'm Captain Anderson. I would like to hire your dogs to help us find criminals. In return, we will pay you $100 per day whenever we use your dogs."

"I don't know if I can do that," Sonia's dad responded. "The dogs belong to Sonia. I will have to ask her about it. I will call you back in a couple of minutes, if that's okay with you." He hung up the phone after Captain Anderson replied affirmatively.

Sonia was curious to know what was going on. "Dad, what was it about?"

"Captain Anderson asked me if he could use your dogs to catch crooks. He is willing to pay you $100 per day. So what do you think, Sonia?"

"Let me ask Mother first," she said.

"It's your choice," her mother said.

Sonia thought it over and said, "I'm fine with it, as long as, he is hiring both dogs at the same time, keeping them together. He'll also have to bring the dogs home before I come back from school."

Her dad called Captain Anderson back and informed him of Sonia's conditions of employment. Captain Anderson agreed and said that he would train the dogs as required. Now Sonia's parents didn't have to struggle for money anymore and her dogs were going to help the police catch crooks and burglars. That made her very happy. Captain Anderson kept his word. Every evening, he brought the dogs back home before Sonia returned from school.

Story 6

The Animal Friend

Omesh was a strong man; he worked hard on the farm and took care of his son Ori. Omesh also took care of a couple of animals that he owned. He milked the cows and collected the eggs from his few chickens. Omesh sold milk and eggs in a local market. As time went by, he grew old and couldn't work on the farm anymore. He needed help. "Ori, come here, my boy," he said.

"Yes, Dad?" Ori stood in front of his dad.

"Sit here."

Ori sat next to his dad.

"Now, I want you to listen to me carefully." Omesh ruffled Ori's hair while talking to him. "From now on, you'll have to take care of our farm and the animals, too."

"Why? Where are you going dad?" Ori asked innocently.

"I'm not going anywhere Ori but I am getting old, I'm too sick. I can't work anymore. That's why I want you to take care of our farm."

"Dad, I'm just a kid, how will I be able to do it?"

"I know, but don't worry; I'll show you what to do."

"Dad, I'll do whatever you want me to do." Ori looked at his dad kindly. Ori loved his dad. His dad would do anything to make Ori happy, too. He was the best dad in the whole wide world.

Once, when Ori was six, he was playing outside, suddenly, a bull charged at Ori, when he was about to strike Ori, his father caught the

bull by his horns and tried to turn him away. But the bull threw his dad to the ground and he broke his hand. Luckily, the bull had been distracted by Ori's dad just enough so that he lost interest in Ori. Omesh was out of work for a couple of weeks while his hand healed, but he didn't mind. In fact, he was just happy that his son was unhurt.

Omesh hugged him and said, "Let's get started." He explained basic things to Ori. Ori learned the basics of farming and taking care of the animals very quickly. He had seen his dad do it for several years. Even though Ori was not really old enough to work on the farm, he was able to shoulder the responsibilities well. As time went by, Ori turned out to be a good farmer. But he still had too much work to do. He also needed to take care of his father, his health was getting worse every week.

One day, when Ori was on his way back home from the market, he saw a stray donkey. The donkey looked weak; it needed shelter. Ori brought the donkey home, washed him and fed him, along with the rest of the animals. Then he helped his dad get settled and finally went to sleep.

The next day, while at the market, Ori was excited to hear about a night school. He knew how badly his dad wanted him to go to school but he could never send him to school because they were too poor and his dad needed helping hand. Now, happily, he enrolled himself as a new student in night school. As it turns out, the price of eggs and milk had gone up and Ori had just enough money for the cost of enrollment.

Ori worked hard on his farm, taking care of the animals and his dad during the day while attending classes at night. Everyone in night school was either very poor or didn't have anyone to support them. All of them were highly motivated and worked hard. Ori's grades were always very high. Teachers loved having him in their classes and all his classmates were very fond of him. They always chose him as their class

monitor and he did an excellent job. When it was time for students to learn about animals, teachers chose Ori to teach them about animals and how to take care of them. His dad was very happy for Ori. Every day, Ori had some interesting stories to tell his dad and his dad always looked forward to them.

One day, Ori said, "Dad I would like to be veterinarian. What do you think about that?"

His dad asked, "What is a veterinarian?"

"I want to be an animal doctor," Ori replied.

"That would be awesome. I know you will be great at it," his dad said.

"How do you know that, Dad?" Ori asked.

"Because you like animals so much and you know how to take care of them already, don't you?" His dad ruffled his hair lovingly.

Ori beamed with delight.

The next day, when Ori told his teachers about his plans, they thought it was a good idea. They encouraged him to study hard to become a veterinarian. For his next birthday, all of his teachers and classmates presented him with different animals. With those gifts came responsibilities. Now he began to take care of pigs, dogs, rabbits, cats and goats, along with his cows, chickens and his donkey. People began to call his farm an Animal Farm, and they nicknamed him an "Animal Friend."

In a few years, he became a very famous veterinarian. He took wonderful care of all the animals that were brought to his clinic. He was the best veterinarian in the area, but more importantly, Ori was the best son to his father. He looked after his father, the man who loved him more than anything else in the world and helped him to become a good human being.

Story 7

The Capture of Ponytail

Mia and Kayla were best friends. They were very excited about their upcoming field trip; they were going to a place where Native Indians lived. This was their first field trip ever. They had heard lots of exciting things about field trips from their older siblings. So they were really looking forward to the experience. They packed their bags and checked them again and again to make sure they didn't forget anything. They didn't sleep at all the night before.

They left early in the morning. They were going to learn about the lifestyle of Native Indians and their ways of tending to animals. Once they reached the forest, the students were instructed to follow their teacher, Mrs. Harper. Of course some of the students took a different path, the path that went through the thick forest. Mrs. Harper had warned the students about the dangers of taking the short cut but some students wanted to reach their first rest stop before everyone else to surprise them.

When Mrs. Harper noticed that some of her students were missing, she immediately took a headcount. "Eight are missing," she sobbed; she began to cry louder than ever. No one knew how to react or what to do. Someone suggested, "Why don't we all go back and find them?"

Mrs. Harper said, "I don't feel safe taking the same route as the missing students because I don't want to put any of you in danger."

"Then what should we do?" the student standing next to her asked.

"I don't know what to do," she cried. "I need help." Her eyes turned red, tears began flowing non-stop.

Mia and Kayla, who were whispering privately, volunteered, "We have an idea."

"What is it?" Mrs. Harper asked anxiously.

"Kayla and I will go back to find the missing students, if you will allow it." Mia looked at the teacher hopefully.

"No, I can't give you permission to do that," Mrs. Harper responded quickly.

"Please, Mrs. Harper, let us go and try before it is too late!" Kayla pleaded.

"I hope you find them quickly and reach our destination before us," the teacher whispered as she gave in.

Mia said, "Mrs. Harper, do you mind carrying our bags for us?"

"I don't mind," Mrs. Harper responded.

Kayla hurriedly opened her bag, took out her emergency kit and put it in her backpack. After closing her bag, she picked up Mia's bag and gave them both to Mrs. Harper. "I wish you all the best!" Mrs. Harper said. "Be safe."

The teacher and other children left the area only after Mia and Kayla were out of their sight. As soon Kayla and Mia entered the forest, monkeys, boars, and several other mysterious animals greeted them, making frightening sounds. Mia said, "I'm scared of these weird animals."

"Me too," Kayla said. "But being scared of them won't help us. We just need to be careful."

"Look at all those birds," Mia said pointing to a flock of colorful birds. "I love birds."

"Me too," Kayla said.

Soon, they came across a spring of crystal clear water. It was tempting. They wanted to play in the water but when they saw alligators and crocodiles crawling around, they got scared and didn't dare go near the water. They quietly went across the spring and through a large wood on the other side. After they entered the thickest part of the forest, where all the trees were very, very tall, they heard a noise that sounded like kids crying. They walked in the direction of the noise on tippy toe. Suddenly, they saw their classmates tied to trees; a man with a ponytail was saying something to them. But Mia and Kayla weren't able to hear him very well. "Why are they tied up? And what is he saying to them?" Mia asked.

"I don't know. But don't talk loud," Kayla whispered. "If he hears us, he will capture us too."

"Look, there is another man coming from behind that tree, do you see him?" Mia asked.

"Yes." Suddenly, Kayla saw a large snake crawling up the tree that they were hiding behind. It scared her to death but she didn't point it out to Mia. She was certain that Mia would scream and they would be captured if she mentioned it. Instead, she said, "Let's move a little closer to hear what they're saying."

"Okay," Mia whispered.

"Be careful," Kayla said, "they must not see us."

When they moved a little closer, they heard kids pleading to be released. The kids looked frightened and very worried. Then they heard ponytail shouting, "You are my hostages and my slaves. If you refuse  to work, I will feed you to the animals! Do you understand?"

The kids nodded.

The other man with the long dirty beard and crooked teeth, said, "Now we will rest here, in the evening we will go to a place where you will work as slaves for my master. Now, I want six of you to massage my master," he pointed his finger in the direction of Ponytail and continued, "and two of you to climb that tree to pick fruit for him to eat after he gets up from his nap." Then he released all the kids and said, "If you try to run away from here, animals will eat you up or I will beat you until you are dead."

"What are we going to do now?" Mia asked quietly.

"Let them rest for now and when the two bad men fall asleep, we will go and rescue our friends," Kayla said.

After both captors fell asleep and began to snore, Mia and Kayla carefully moved forward. When their friends saw Mia and Kayla, they were about to shout in excitement. Kayla immediately placed her finger on her lips and her friends understood what she wanted them to do. They kept quiet as instructed.

Kayla carefully opened her emergency kit, quietly removed two bottles of liquid glue, took off the lids and gave one bottle to Mia and the other to Smarty, Mrs. Harper's daughter. After showing them what she wanted them to do with the glue, Kayla picked up a pack of red chili powder and held onto it. Then she silently gave them the signal to go forward.

Mia and Smarty quickly poured the liquid on the two men's faces. As soon as they woke up, Kayla threw the chili powder in their eyes. When their eyes started burning, they tried to rub them, but they couldn't do it. Their hands got stuck to their faces, they began to jump all over the place just like monkeys. The funny thing was, they couldn't even cry or ask for help, their lips were also stuck.

Later, Mia used lots of glue to stick Ponytail's hair to the tree. After tying Ponytail and his assistant to the tree, Kayla shouted, "Pick up your bags fast and let's run away from here." Immediately, all of them picked up their bags and ran as fast as they could.

Mrs. Harper and all their classmates

were mesmerized when Smarty narrated the whole incident, especially how Mia and Kayla rescued them. When the Native Indians heard the story, they immediately ran to the spot, along with Kayla and Mia, and captured the crooks who had been stealing kids for years.

Kayla and Mia were rewarded for their brave act. The Indians held a feast in celebration of their bravery. Since then, they have been given the title of "The brave girls."

Story 8

The Little Helper

Grace liked helping people. She didn't care if she got anything in return. She just wanted to help. She came from a very poor family, her parents had very little but they were kind-hearted and cared for others. Grace was just like her parents, kind and helpful. One Sunday, when she heard that their neighbor, Mrs. Luana, was very sick, she immediately went over to check on her. She knocked on the door, a hoarse voice answered, "Come in, come in." Immediately, upon entering, she noticed that Mrs. Luana wasn't poor. She had a fine house. Mrs. Luana wasn't friendly to anyone in the neighborhood so no one ever visited her. She lived alone and gave everyone the impression that she was very aloof. Grace liked Mrs. Luana's house very much. The furniture was nicely arranged and looked very classy. The marble looked rich and shiny. Grace wanted to touch the marble, but she remembered that she hadn't gone there to have fun or do anything silly. She was there to check on Mrs. Luana. Looking around, she saw Mrs. Luana lying on the couch. "Are you feeling alright Mrs. Luana?" Grace asked softly.

"Yes, just a little sick, that's all," she replied painfully. To Grace, Mrs. Luana didn't look just a little sick. She looked very sick.

"Is it okay if I go and get you some water from your kitchen faucet?" Grace asked.

"That is very kind of you," Mrs. Luana said slowly.

Grace went to the kitchen and brought some water for Mrs. Luana. When Mrs. Luana tried to hold onto the glass, her hands trembled, water spilled all over her. Grace helped her to drink the water by helping her with the glass. Then Mrs. Luana asked Grace to get her medication from the refrigerator. Grace brought her the medication she needed. "But don't you have to eat something before you take your medication?" Grace asked her kindly.

"I do. But there is nothing in the house to eat and I haven't cooked in days, nor I have been to market recently," she responded in a barely audible voice.

"I could bring you something to eat from my house?" Grace asked.

"Oh, thank you, I would love to have something to eat before I take my medication." Mrs. Luana looked at Grace hopefully.

"I'll be right back," and out the door she ran.

Grace looked for her mother, her mother wasn't around. So she looked around for something to eat for Mrs. Luana. When she couldn't find anything in the house, she began to cry because she realized that they were so poor they didn't have anything to give to the sick neighbor to eat. When her mother arrived, she asked, "Are you alright, Grace?"

Grace couldn't answer her question, she continued crying.

"What's wrong, my dear? Is Mrs. Luana okay?"

"No mother, she isn't doing well at all. She needs something to eat right away before she takes her medication. But there was nothing in her house to eat. I promised to bring her something to eat. But there is nothing in our house either. Now, what should I do?" she continued sobbing.

"Don't worry, Grace," her mother said, "look at this, I have four eggs and a loaf of bread for you and your father. I just got back from the market."

"What about you, Mom? What are you going to eat?" Grace asked.

"I'm fasting today. I fast a couple of days a week." Her mother averted her eyes. Grace knew that her mother never fasted on Sundays. Whenever there wasn't enough food in the house, her mother would tell everyone that she was fasting. It was clear to Grace that her mother didn't have enough money to buy more eggs or anything, so she had decided to fast even on Sunday now.

"Now, don't waste time worrying. Let's make an omelet for Mrs. Luana so you can take it to her before it's too late for her to take her medication." Her mother hurriedly stepped into the kitchen.

Mrs. Luana wasn't able to lift her hand to eat on her own. So Grace fed her with the fork and spoon as soon as she got back to her house. Grace helped her to take her medication as soon as she was done with her food. Mrs. Luana felt a little better after that. "Thank you, Grace! I think you should go now. Your parents must be waiting for you," Mrs. Luana said kindly.

"Yes, I do need to go now, but I'll come back with my mother to check on you before I go to bed," Grace said.

Later that night, Grace and her mother went to check on Mrs. Luana. She seemed to be tired but was happy to see Grace and her mother. Grace's mother mopped all the floors in Mrs. Luana's house and changed the bed sheets and pillow covers for her. Then she helped Mrs. Luana get into her bed. From that day on, Grace would take care of her. She would buy her groceries, fetch water from the well and feed her. But Grace knew that Mrs. Luana was getting worse, after all, she was eighty-seven years old. Her face was so pale, she looked like a ghost and she barely said a word.

Then one day she said something to Grace. "Grace, bring me a piece of paper and a pencil, please." Grace brought her paper and pencil and Mrs. Luana scribbled something on the paper. She folded it up, then told Grace, "Please take this to Mr. Zambo, he lives just two houses away from us." Grace took the envelope to Mr. Zambo. He asked her to wait until he gave her another envelope. Mrs. Luana opened the envelope, signed the paper that was inside and folded it again. "Grace, keep this with you and open this only after I'm gone." Grace didn't like the idea of Mrs. Luana going anywhere. She was happy taking care of her. Grace's mother often came over to help Mrs. Luana bathe; she also cooked fresh food for her.

Feeling sad, Grace put food and water on the table for Mrs. Luana and left. Grace came back the next day to check on Mrs. Luana, she was sleeping. Grace looked in the refrigerator. It was empty, except for half a gallon of milk.

"I think I should go to the market," Grace said to herself. She picked up some change lying on the desk and went to the market. There weren't a lot of things she needed to get so she was done buying the groceries quickly; she went back to Mrs. Luana's house and arranged the refrigerator. Then she went to see

Mrs. Luana but she realized that Mrs. Luana wasn't breathing. It scared her. She immediately ran back to our house to get her mother to check on Mrs. Luana. Her mother said, "She is dead, sorry Grace."

"So sad," Grace whispered, "I hope she didn't cry." Then she remembered the envelope. Grace opened it. It was Mrs. Luana's will. She had given everything she owned to Grace. At the bottom it said,

Thank you for taking care of me; you are a great little helper.

Everyone heard about this and they followed in her footsteps. They started helping others. Grace's family was no longer poor. Everyone started calling her, "The Little Helper."

Story 9

Looks Don't Matter; the Heart Does

Kristina was a forty-year-old woman who just didn't fit in anywhere because of her looks. Everyone said she was odd looking. Actually, everyone called her the 'ugly old duckling.' Even when she was in school, she was nicknamed 'Ugly – Pigly.' No one wanted to be anywhere near her nor would anyone give her a job even though she was well educated and very clean. "Out!" the men often screamed when Kristina looked for work. She walked away quietly every time.

"May I babysit your children?" she asked a woman politely.

"No!" The woman screamed. "You're the ugliest old hag I have ever seen! Get away from my door right away." Poor Kristina wasn't welcomed anywhere.

She was very sad; she missed her husband, Dante, very much. He had passed away a couple of years ago. He had known her from their school days. Her looks never mattered to him at all. To him, she was the most beautiful woman he had ever met. But after his death, her world changed. She needed money to take care of her two beautiful daughters; they looked just like her. They were the best people to be around, but no one thought about that. People talked more about their looks than their acts of kindness.

One day, Kristina was walking by a well when she saw a small child, about three-years-old, trying to reach for the bucket. Before Kristina could stop him, he fell in the well. Even though she wasn't a good swimmer, she jumped in. Thankfully, she was just in time. She grabbed the child and climbed up the well. "Tanku," the little boy said to Kristina, he kissed her on her cheek. Kristina

could not stop crying. The child's parents came rushing over, and when they saw the sopping wet boy in Kristina's hands, they immediately snatched him from her and pushed her away. The boy's mother said, "How dare you touch my baby and pour cold water on him?" Before Kristina could say anything, the child's father said, "Wait! Let me get the police; they will teach you a lesson." Soon, the police arrived and arrested her. A handicapped neighbor had seen the child fall into the well. He also saw Kristina jump in and save the child. He reached the spot, pulling his damaged leg along as rapidly as he could. "Hold on there," he said, breathing heavily.

The police officer said, "You better stay out of this."

"How can I ignore this when you are arresting an innocent woman?" the gentleman asked angrily.

"What do you mean by innocent?" The officer looked at Kristina angrily.

"Officer, you are making a big mistake. This poor woman saved that child. I witnessed the whole incident. Look at her! Doesn't see look innocent to you?"

"No, she doesn't," the officer said unkindly.

"I pity you," the man said. "Why don't you ask the child what happened?"

The officer moved close to the child and asked, "What happened? Who poured water on you?"

"I --- in the well," he said sweetly, pointing his finger inside the well.

"Did this woman do anything to you?" the officer continued.

"Yes," the child responded.

"She pushed you, didn't she?" The officer made an action of pushing him with both hands.

"No," the child said. "She picked me up and I kissed her."

The officer warned the child's parents to watch him closely and left without apologizing to Kristina. Then the couple walked away, feeling ashamed of themselves. The little boy waved to Kristina and said, "Bye bye."

The handicapped gentleman introduced himself to Kristina, "I'm Jack. I'm a police officer and I'm currently on leave. I was involved in a fatal accident. My wife died in that accident, so I moved here recently."

Kristina just looked at him.

"I need some help since I'm not able to move around very well. Would you mind helping me?"

"I'll be glad to do any work for you, sir," Kristina said joyfully.

"When can you start?" he asked.

"…Right away." She helped him walk back to his apartment.

Thereafter, she began doing all sorts of work for him, cooking, doing the dishes, cleaning the house, washing clothes and even going to the bank for him. Her daughters came to his apartment daily. They called him sir, but he told them to call him uncle. He loved their company. He would buy lots of toys, clothes and books for them. After a couple of months, he began to walk on his own and started working for a local police station.

On his birthday, he did not invite anyone except Kristina and her two daughters. They had lots of fun together. He had lots of food that the girls liked. They enjoyed the food and the cake was delicious. When Kristina and her daughters were about to leave, Jack stopped them and said, "Would you like to stay here forever?" The girls liked the idea very much but Kristina didn't know what to say. She seemed to be confused. So Jack walked up to her, got down on one knee and proposed, "Would you marry me?"

"No," Kristina responded.

"…Why not?"

"I'm so ugly, you are so handsome. I'm not a good match for you," she began to move away.

"Kristina, you are the most beautiful woman I ever know. You have the purest heart and I really love you. I love your daughters as if they were my own."

Her daughters said, "Mommy, please marry Uncle Jack."

The following spring, Kristina and Jack got married and lived happily ever after. Her daughters were very happy with their stepdad. He took good care of them just as if they were his own daughters.

Later, Kristina started her own childcare center and the first child who came to her center was the same little boy she had saved from drowning. His parents said they were sorry and were truly ashamed of their behavior. Slowly, things changed. All the kids in her childcare loved her and their parents did too.

Story 10

Two Wrongs Don't Make a Right

Angelo never saw his mother. She died the day he was born. His father never married again. He was afraid that a new wife might treat his sons poorly. Hunter, Angelo's older brother (only by one year) behaved like he was much older and stronger than Angelo. He would not allow anyone to bully his baby brother. Hunter didn't want to fight anyone or meddle in anyone's business, but he couldn't tolerate anyone harassing his brother.

In school, the children teased them often because they were poor and wore the same torn uniforms five days a week. They did not bring any food to eat during lunch break. They were very poor. They didn't even have enough notebooks or other school supplies so Angelo used Hunter's books since he was only one year older.

Their dad, Blake, owned a cow. He would milk her early in the morning and sell the milk at a local market. When he wasn't milking his cow, he worked as a farm laborer. Though he was poor, he was kind and generous. He was nice to everyone and he loved his sons a lot. He wanted his sons to go to school, to learn to read and write and find jobs to make a living. He didn't want them to be illiterate like himself, having to work on other people's farms for very little money. He knew what his sons liked. Hunter loved to sing; Angelo's passion was drawing. He would encourage both his sons to practice what they were good at. He would watch Angelo paint for hours.

Angelo would always draw pictures of his mother and he drew them very well. There weren't any real pictures of his mother so he imagined what he thought she looked like as he was drawing. Angelo wished someone had taken his mother's picture when she was still alive. He would have given anything in exchange for a real picture – anything really! Most of his drawings portrayed a cow, his brother while singing, his father, and his mother, working around their hut. Some of them pictured Angelo sitting on her lap. His brother would argue with him, "How come you never picture me sitting on our mother's lap?" Angelo would reply, "I don't know. I guess I need her more than you do." His brother would give up and hug him. He would often draw their hut as if it were a palace - the most beautiful place in the world.

Angelo and Hunter were mindful of their father's struggle so they would always behave. At a very early age, they began to milk the cow and sell the milk. Even when the other children teased them, they would not complain to their father about the other children. On their way to school and back, a gang, Damaged Brain, harassed them frequently. But Angelo and Hunter would always walk away quietly. One day, the gang's leader, Damian, pushed Angelo when they were on a hill, Angelo almost fell into the valley, luckily his brother grabbed his hand in time and saved him. "Enough is enough," Hunter shouted, he attacked Damian. Hunter hammered on Damian until Damian fainted. His friends ran away and hid. Angelo ran down the hill,

brought back some water and helped Damien drink it. Until then, he could barely catch breath

When they told their dad about the incident, he became upset with them and said, "Remember, two wrongs don't make a right."

Unfortunately, even after that incident, the gang didn't stop harassing Hunter and Angelo. The poor brothers didn't want to fight anyone, so they began to take a different route to school. The new route was rougher and longer than the regular way. When the gang found out that the brothers were taking a different route, they followed them. One day, tired of the harassment, the brothers complained to their teachers, but the teachers didn't dare to punish the bad boys. That evening, on their way back home, Damian caught Hunter by his jaw, looked into his mouth and said, "First, we'll remove all your teeth and then the Damaged Brain gang will stomp on your brain as well as your brother's." Somehow, Hunter managed to free himself from Damian's grip. "Run! Angelo run," Hunter shouted. They both ran as fast as they could. Damian and his

gang began chasing them, taking shortcuts. Suddenly, Damian cried out, "Please help me, please help me, I've been bitten by a snake. I don't want to die." Everyone turned back, no one knew what to do. Looking at him, they realized he was dying. Angelo said to himself, "Let him die. He deserves it." But a moment later, he remembered his dad's words, 'two wrongs don't make a right'. He immediately

changed his mind, moved forward and bit Damian on the exact spot where the snake had bitten him. He sucked the poisonous blood out and spit it on the ground and then allowed Damian's blood to flow freely. The other kids didn't know what he was doing, but his brother knew and he was worried for Angelo too. Hunter and Angelo picked up Damian and carried him to a doctor's clinic. The doctor saved his life. Later, the doctor told Damian's parents that if Angelo hadn't done what he did and the brothers hadn't brought Damian to his clinic on time, Damian would be dead right now.

The next day, Damian visited Angelo and his brother in their hut and said, "I'm sorry. Please forgive me for being bad to you and accept me as your friend." Transformed, Damian changed the name of his gang from Damaged Brain to Helping Eleven.

Made in the USA
Charleston, SC
08 June 2014